From the Association
Dec. 20, '94

REPORTS

OF THE

COMMITTEE ON TAXATION

— OF THE —

CITIZENS' ASSOCIATION

OF CHICAGO.

Made September 26th, 1874, and December 3d, 1874.

CHICAGO:
PRINTED BY DIRECTION OF THE EXECUTIVE COMMITTEE OF THE CITIZENS' ASSOCIATION.
1874.

FIRST REPORT.

To the Executive Committee of the Citizens' Association of Chicago:

The Committee on Taxation appointed by you, beg leave to submit the following preliminary Report:

The subject of taxation is so vast and complex that it would be the work of years rather than of days to examine carefully and discuss fully its many branches and the various questions connected with it.

But there are so many and such serious defects in the tax system now in operation in Chicago that your committee deem it advisable to call attention at once to some of its most palpable evils, and to suggest remedies for them, reserving more intricate matters for the fuller consideration which they demand.

UNEQUAL ASSESSMENTS OF VALUATION.

The gravest of these evils and that which works the greatest injustice, is the wide inequality in the assessments of valuation, particularly those upon which state, county and town taxes are based. In consequence of this inequality, some individuals pay a two, three, and in some instances ten-fold greater tax in proportion to the real value of their property, than other owners in the same town. That this is not an over statement, the following instances, carefully verified by your committee, will testify. They all occur in the assessment for 1873, upon which taxes are now being paid.

In one town its Assessor assessed one very valuable piece of improved business property at a little less than *six per cent.* of its real value, another large tract, docked, and used for lumber yards at *twenty per cent.* of its real value, and still another large and valuable property, built up with residences, at *ninety per cent.* of its real value. The Assessor in another town valued a piece of improved business property at *six per cent.* of its value, a residence at *sixteen per cent.* of its value, and a vacant lot at *sixty per cent.* of its value. These towns are both situated within the city limits, but in one of the towns adjoining the city, while two tracts of land were assessed at only *four* and *five per cent.* of their respective values, other tracts were assessed at nearly, if not quite, their full values. And in one of the remoter towns in Cook county, the Assessor valued all of the land in it at a uniform rate per acre, although he must have known that the value of the farms in that town varied from thirty to one hundred and fifty dollars per acre. These are not isolated instances, and your committee believe that they fairly illustrate the existing modes of assessment for purposes of taxation in many, if not all, of the towns in this county, the records of which will show numerous similar cases of excessive over, and under, valuation.

NO REMEDY FROM COUNTY BOARD.

The County Board of Equalization furnishes no remedy for this state of things. So numerous and great are these discrepancies that to adjust a single assessment equitably between the individual property owners in this county, would require the Equalizing Board to be in session an entire year. Nor would justice then be done unless the members of the board were familiar with the true value of every piece of property in the county, a thing which is simply impossible with our present revenue machinery.

It is possible for this county board to equalize the assessment of valuation for town, county and state purposes, between the different towns with some approach to fairness. Yet in so doing, the injustice to individuals is only aggravated. It was ascertained that in some of the towns in this county the assessment of real estate for a particular year did not average more than ten per cent. of the real value, while in other towns for the same year it was sixty per cent.

Assuming that the average assessment of realty for the whole county was forty per cent. of the true value for that year, equalization between the two classes of towns designated can be made by multiplying the assessment in the first by four, and reducing it by one-third in the other. But in the first class of towns the property of many individuals was assessed at thirty per cent. of its value, and that of others at only five per cent., making the average valuation of the town ten per cent. of what the property in it was really worth. When you multiply by four to equalize between the two classes of towns, you make some owners pay upon one hundred and twenty per cent, of their property, or one-fifth more than it is worth, while those assessed at five per cent. originally, still pay only upon one-half of the proper value. And when the State Board of Equalization repeats this proceeding upon a large scale in its attempts to adjust the valuation as between counties, the wrong in many cases, becomes enormous.

The *vital error* lies in the inequality in the original assessment of valuation.

NO HOPE OF RELIEF UNDER PRESENT SYSTEM.

There is little hope of relief from this great wrong while the present method of selecting the men who make these original assessments continues.

The assessors chosen at town meetings are usually ignorant of the duties to be performed, and not always incorruptible. And even if they were competent and honest, it would be impossible for them in any of the three towns in the city of Chicago, to make a fair assessment in the limited time within which they are required by law to do their work.

JUDICIOUS LEGISLATION THE ONLY REMEDY.

Your committee believe that the only adequate remedy for these evils will be found in judicious legislation by the State.

In the first place, the township organization, in Cook county, should be done away with, it being, in this city at any rate, utterly useless and *vicious*. Then there should be but one valuation of property, on the basis of which, all taxes for city, county and State should be levied.

This would dispense with one-half of the present machinery and expense in conducting this business. A Supervisor of Revenue for the county should be appointed, whose duty it should be to procure perfect maps and plats of all the lands, blocks, lots and sub-lots in the county, upon a large scale, and a complete set of books in which should be entered the character of the improvements upon each tract or lot, and the date and consideration of one or more of its most recent transfers. Where practicable these data should be noted upon the face of the maps. With this information before him, the Revenue Supervisor could readily compare the assessment with the real value of each piece of property, and note the addition or reduction necessary in each case, to bring it to the average valuation. His conclusions he should be required to report to the Equalizing Board, which should have the power to confirm them without notice to owners of property as to which changes may be made. But these books should be open to the inspection of any tax payer on every business day in the year, that all may see that no injustice is done.

This Revenue Officer should appoint all of his assistant assessors and clerks, and be held strictly accountable for their official acts. His term of office should be for a reasonably long period of time, he being subject, of course, to removal for malfeasance in office. The more experience had by such officer and his assistants, the more valuable would be their services, and each succeeding year would enable them to more and more nearly approach to exact justice to each tax payer.

Under our State Constitution, laws must be general in their application, but if the proposed plan for obtaining an honest and fair valuation of taxable property is not desired by the less populous counties, the system can be confined to such counties as have a population exceeding a given number, which can be made so large as to apply only to the county of Cook, if no others wish to adopt it.

SUBJECT OF FUTURE REPORTS.

The defects in our General Revenue Law which affect State taxation, and its provisions relating to the State Board of Equalization, the questions of general or special assessments for local improvements, and direct or indirect taxation, and such other topics as may come within the province of this committee may be the subjects of future reports, should it seem advisable.

Respectfully submitted,

A. J. GALLOWAY,
E. G. MASON,
ROBERT LAW.

Chicago, Sept. 26, 1874.

SECOND REPORT.

To the Executive Committee of the Citizens' Association of Chicago:

The Committee on Taxation appointed by you made a preliminary report on the 26th of September last, in which some of the most obvious evils of the present system of levying and collecting taxes in our city were pointed out, and remedies for the same were suggested. That report was re-committed to the Committee on October 15, with instructions to make a further report as to the best and most feasible methods, in their judgment, of carrying out their suggestions. Since that time the Committee have carefully considered their former propositions, have had before them the views in writing of different persons conversant with the subject, and have availed themselves of the best assistance which they could obtain, as will more fully appear herein. It will be remembered that

THE REFORMS PROPOSED

were the abolition of township organization and uniform valuation of property under the control of a single officer, appointed for such a term and with such powers as would most judiciously accomplish this result. Taking these suggestions in order, your Committee would observe that upon mature reflection they are fully convinced of the propriety and importance of their recommendation, that township organization should be done away with. Recent events confirm this conclusion, if confirmation were necessary. We characterized this system in our previous report as utterly useless and vicious. We might add that it is a great and unnecessary expense, that it stands in the way of almost any tax reform, and that by its abolition we can secure a system more economical and effective, and under which the desired improvements in our modes of taxation can more readily be obtained. It remains only to determine whether there are any legal obstacles to making this change, and if not, in what way it can be brought about. There has been so much discussion upon the subject, and it is in some respects so involved, that, to properly understand it, it seems advisable to briefly sketch the history of

TOWNSHIP ORGANIZATION IN COOK COUNTY.

Under the constitution of 1848, two classes of counties existed in Illinois. The first class comprised those counties not adopting township organization, which were not divided into towns, and in which all the business of each part of the county was transacted by the County Court. The second class comprised those counties adopting township organization, which were divided into townships or towns, each of which was a body corporate, managing its own affairs and with its own officers, comprising a Supervisor, Town Clerk, Assessor, Collector, Justice of the Peace, and other minor officials. And in counties of the second class general county affairs were managed by a Board of Supervisors, made up of the Supervisors elected from the several towns and city wards in the county. Each county was a body corporate by itself, whether divided into towns or not. Cook county belonged to the second class, namely, those adopting township organization, and at the time of the assembling of the last Constitutional Convention its citizens were dissatisfied with its Board of Supervisors. There was a general desire for a change in the management of the general county affairs, and our delegates were anxious to bring it about. In the Convention there was little or no discussion upon the matter, all propositions relating to it being referred to the Cook county delegation. The result of their deliberations, which the Convention adopted, was the section establishing a Board of Fifteen Commissioners to manage the affairs of Cook county. All of the provisions of our present constitution which relate to county government are comprised in article ten, and are as follows:

COUNTY GOVERNMENT.

SECTION 5. The General Assembly shall provide, by general law, for township organization, under which any county may organize whenever a majority of the legal voters of such county, voting at any general election, shall so determine, and whenever any county shall adopt township organization, so much of this constitution as provides for the management of the fiscal concerns of the said county by the board of county commissioners, may be dispensed with, and the affairs of said county may be transacted in such manner as the general assembly may provide. And in any county that shall have adopted a township organization, the question of continuing the same may be submitted to a vote of the electors of such county, at a general election, in the manner that now is or may be provided by law; and if a majority of all the votes cast upon that question shall be against township organization, then such organization shall cease in said county; and all laws in force in relation to counties not having township organization, shall immediately take effect and be in force in such county. No two townships shall have the same name, and the day of holding the annual township meeting shall be uniform throughout the State.

SEC. 6. At the first election of county judges under this constitution, there shall be elected in each of the counties in this state, not under township organization, three officers who shall be styled "The Board of county commissioners," who shall hold sessions for the transaction of county business as shall be provided by law. One of said commissioners shall hold his office for one year, one for two years, and one for three years, to be determined by lot; and every year thereafter one such officer shall be elected in each of said counties for the term of three years.

SEC. 7. The county affairs of Cook county shall be managed by a board of commissioners of fifteen persons, ten of whom shall be elected from the city of Chicago, and five from towns outside of said city, in such manner as shall be provided by law.

The common understanding of the effect of these provisions has been that so far as Cook county is concerned township organization was continued therein as previously existing, but with the substitution of a Board of Fifteen Commissioners for the old Board of Supervisors. It is well known that this was the only object at that time desired to be accomplished by the people of Cook county, and all of our delegates to the Convention whom your committee have been able to see, agree in the statement that this was the sole intention of the Cook county delegation and of the Convention.

Upon this view all concerned have acted since the adoption of the constitution of 1870, and our Legislature seems to recognize it as the correct one, in the act of April 22, 1871, which provides that "the Cook county Commissioners shall have the same powers, duties, etc., *as prescribed by law for the Board of Supervisors*," and in the revision of 1874, which provides that "all laws applicable to the County Clerks of other counties *under township organization*, shall be applicable to the County Clerk of Cook county." R. S. 1874, p. 312, §§ 60–63. And your committtee believe this to be the present status of the system of township organization in the county of Cook.

TOWNSHIP ORGANIZATION CAN BE ABOLISHED.

It follows, therefore, in our opinion, that it is as competent now for the people of the county to abolish this system as it was under the constitution of 1848. We are aware that the opinion is entertained by some that the system in question was in fact abolished by the constitution of 1870 in this county. This proceeds upon the assumption that there are but two classes of counties recognized in the new constitution, one under the commissioner system, and one under township organization; and that Cook county, being placed under the government of Commissioners, must wholly belong to the commissioner system class, and can therefore have nothing to do with township organization, which by implication must have been abolished within its limits. The error here lies in overlooking the fact that the constitution nowhere limits the number of classes of counties, and does practically create a third class, in which the old township organization was continued, except as to the Board of Supervisors, for which a substitute was provided, to which third class Cook county alone belongs. The absence of any evidence of intention to abolish township organization here, and of any express provision upon the subject in the constitution, and the recognition of its continuance in the provision that five of Commissioners shall be elected from the towns outside of the the city, are also reasons conclusive to our minds as to the incorrectness of this opinion.

An argument has also been made to show that the existing

condition of things in this regard was, by the constitution, rendered irrevocable. This reasoning recognizes the continuance of the township system in Cook county by the constitution, and finding no express provision for its abolition here, infers that it cannot be done away with. It is urged that section five of article ten provides that when township organization ceases in a county, all laws in force in counties not having township organization shall take effect, and that section six provides that counties not under township organization shall have three Commissioners, of whom, after the first election, one shall be elected each year, and hold office for three years, and that the laws enacted to carry out these sections make the same provisions. Hence, as Cook county has already a Board of Fifteen Commissioners, it is argued that the change provided by the constitution, being from township organization to a government by three commissioners, cannot be made here; that, therefore, sections five and six have no application in Cook county, and that section seven finally disposes of the matter for us. But it seems to your committee that the accepted rule of construction which requires all of the provisions of a statute relating to one subject to be so read as to be consistent and harmonious throughout furnishes a sufficient answer to this theory.

The three sections referred to, can be read together without violence to their spirit or language, so as to entirely harmonize, by treating section seven as a modification of sections five and six, so far as Cook county is concerned. Their plain meaning, then, will be that township organization may be abolished in any county which has adopted it, including Cook county, and the laws concerning counties not under township organization will come in force, except so far as they are modified in the case of Cook county by section seven. It seems a necessary inference, from the fact that the constitution has made the government of Cook county an exception to the general provisions governing counties, that all such general requirements when applied to this county must be construed in accordance with the special provisions relating to it. Hence a vote of the people of Cook county, at a general election, dispensing with township organization, would not vest the control of the county and township affairs in three Commissioners, provided for other counties, but in the fifteen Commissioners provided in Cook county. It is possible that it may be well to obtain an amendment to the existing statute upon township organization, to remove any doubt as to the immediate succession of our present Board of Commissioners to the present town governments, in case the township system is discontinued. But we do not consider any legislation necessary to enable the people of our county to effect such discontinuance, and as to the

METHOD OF ABOLISHING TOWNSHIP ORGANIZATIONS,

we are glad to be able to submit herewith an opinion on this subject, kindly prepared at their request, by the chairman of your committee on municipal organization, M. F. Tuley, Esq., whose views must carry with them the greatest weight.

OPINION BY M. F. TULEY, ESQ.

To A. J. Galloway, Chairman Committee on Taxation:

You ask my opinion as to the best and most feasible way of getting rid of township organization in Chicago. Every person who has given the subject any attention must admit that a large city has no more need of township organization than a common road wagon has of five wheels. It is not only a great burden upon the tax payers, but it has become an intolerable nuisance. The General Assembly of the State made an attempt at its last session to abolish the most objectionable feature of it, to-wit: the voting of money for town purposes by the annual town meetings, by conferring the power to fix the amounts to be expended by the towns upon the Board of County Commissioners; but, in my opinion, as long as the township organization system is maintained, any law which takes away from the people or the town authorities the power to appropriate and levy the town taxes, is unconstitutional and void. It is difficult to perceive how township organization can be made one thing in cities and a different thing in the country, and not be subject to constitutional objections. After mature reflection I can perceive no way in which, by amendment of the present law, or otherwise, township organization can be maintained for any purpose in large cities, and at the same time the voters of the towns, or the town authorities, be deprived of the power to impose taxes for town purposes. The new constitution of 1870 guarantees the right to all counties to discontinue township organization if the voters desire to do so. It provides by Sec. 5, Art. 10, "that in any county that shall have adopted township organization, the question of continuing the same may be submitted to a vote of the electors of such county at a general election in the manner that now is or may be provided by law." The General Assembly in the township organization act in force March 4, 1874, made the following provisions for an election upon the question of discontinuing township organization:

"SECTION 1. ART. 2. Upon the petition of at least one-fifth of the legal voters of any county having adopted township organization, to be ascertained by the vote cast at the last preceding Presidential election, the county board shall cause to be submitted to the voters of such county, at the next general election, the question of the continuance of township organization, to be voted on by ballots written or printed, or partly written or printed, 'For the continuance of township organization,' or 'Against the continuance of township organization, notice to be given and the votes to be canvassed and returns made in like manner as in this Act provided in reference to a vote on the adoption of township organization.

"SEC. 2. If it shall appear by the returns of said election that a majority of the votes cast on that question at said election are against the continuance of township organization, then such organization shall cease in said county as soon as a county board is elected and qualified; and all laws relating to counties not under township organization shall be applicable to such county the same as if township organization had never been adopted in it."

A question has been raised as to whether the law in question, and also the constitutional provision quoted, are applicable to Cook county; but it must be borne in mind that the constitution itself, so far as the county board of fifteen commissioners is concerned, makes an exception in favor of Cook county. It is not to be presumed that the framers of the constitution intended to except Cook county from the benefit of the provision authorizing counties to discontinue township organization, nor that the General Assembly did not intend to include Cook county in the law passed to carry out that constitutional provision. I am satisfied that no such absurd construction would be placed thereon by the courts.

An election can be had, and township organization can be discontinued, in my opinion, under the law as it now stands. A discontinuance of township organization may be objected to by some of the country towns; but as many of them, like Hyde Park, Cicero, Lake View, and others, are acting under special charters, or under the general incorporation act for cities and villages, and as most of the other towns are sufficiently densely populated to enable them to organize as villages under that act, no great opposition from the outside towns should be expected. In Cicero and Lake, and probably other towns acting under special charters, the supervisor and town assessor and collector are all, or some one or more of them, made *ex-officio* members of the board of trustees of the town.

It should be seen to that a law be passed to prevent any difficulty arising in such towns by the discontinuance of township organization throughout the county. When township organization shall be abolished in Cook county, the county will come under the laws applicable to counties not under township organization. One great benefit from the change will be that we will have but one assessor for the whole county, and the great irregularities in the assessment of property necessarily resulting from the great number of assessors under the township organization system will be avoided. The sheriff will be *ex-officio* county collector. There will be great economy in dispensing with the township organization system. I might mention also the fact that no appropriation could be made for the erection of a court house or other public building without first submitting the same to a vote of the people of the county.

Respectfully, M. F. TULEY.

Your committee will only add, in this connection, that the total vote of this county cast at the last preceding presidential election was, in round numbers, 50,300, and that it will therefore be necessary to present a petition signed by at least 10,060 of the legal voters of this county to the county board, to obtain a submission to the voters of the county at the next general election of the question of the continuance of township organization. Such election will take place on the first Tuesday after the first Monday in November in the year 1875.

UNIFORM VALUATION OF PROPERTY UNDER ONE REVENUE OFFICER.

The second suggestion of your committee in their previous report was that there should be but one valuation of property, on the basis of which all taxes for city, county and State purposes should be levied, and that there should be a single revenue officer, or assessor, for the county, with power to appoint assistant assessors and clerks, holding office for a reasonably long period, whose duty it should be to procure perfect maps of all real estate in the county, and to keep a complete set of books showing the character of the improvements on each tract or lot and the date and consideration of one or more of its most recent transfers, and by whom all assessments should be made, subject to the revision of the county equalization board. The abolition of township organization is the first step to this end. A return to the other system gives us one assessor for the whole county, which office, in counties not under township organization, is, under the present law, held by the county treasurer, *ex-officio*. To secure from this officer the uniform and accurate valuation desired, we should deem it advisable to ask for legislation; and the law defining his duties, and fixing his term of office in Cook county, can be made to take effect when the people of the county have decided by a legal vote to dispense with the existing system.

PROPER LEGISLATION CAN BE OBTAINED UNDER THE CONSTITUTION.

It is the opinion of some able lawyers, that the county of Cook, having been excepted from some of the general provisions which apply to counties and townships in the rest of the State, is therefore not subject to the restriction contained in the sixth clause of Sec. 22, Art. IV., of the constitution of 1870, that the constitution recognizes the fact that the county of Cook, containing a great commercial city, must have special provisions for its government; and that we are fully justified in asking and obtaining any special legislation which the peculiarities of our position or condition as a municipality may require. It is very much to be regretted that a power so essential to the well-being of municipal corporations should have been made to depend upon implied powers; and an amendment to the State constitution, expressly exempting all municipal corporations from this oppressive restriction, would have a very salutary effect. Two or three States which have revised their constitutions since the adoption of ours, have—in following our provisions against special legislation—had the wisdom to exempt their municipal corporations from this restricting clause.

But to avoid all risk or uncertainty in the premises, your committee deem it advisable to recommend that the legislation asked for be in accordance with the suggestions in their preliminary report of September 26th.

LEVY OF CITY TAXES ON COUNTY VALUATION.

When a single assessment for State and county purposes has been established in the method proposed, our city revenue can also be based upon it, and thus a uniform valuation for all purposes of taxation made complete. The general act for the incorporation of cities and villages, approved April 10, 1872, provides that the city council may levy and assess the amount of the yearly appropriations upon the property within the city subject to taxation, as the same is assessed for State and county purposes for the current year. The tax so assessed shall be collected and enforced in the same manner, and by the same officers, as State and county taxes, and shall be paid over by the officers collecting the same to the treasurer of the city. R. S. 1874, p. 231. The act in regard to the assessment of property and the levy and collection of taxes by incorporated cities, approved April 15th, 1873, provides, however, for an assessor and collector in incorporated cities, to be elected by the people, whose duties shall be prescribed by ordinance (R. S. 1874, p. 254); but it also provides that the city council shall have power at any time, by ordinance to elect to levy the annual appropriations upon the assessment for State and county taxes, and in such case to abolish the offices of city assessor and city collector. (R. S. 1874, p. 259.) The latter act, popularly known as "Bill Number 300," is obnoxious for various reasons, and having already been held to be inoperative, should be repealed. In case of its repeal, and of the incorporation of our city as now contemplated, under the general act first referred to, then our city revenue will be based upon the State and county valuation. In case it is not repealed, it is still optional with our city council to levy the annual appropriations upon the State and county valuation, and in that event steps should be taken to bring about this action on the part of the council, or to secure legislation to compel it.

CONSOLIDATION NO REMEDY FOR EVILS OF TOWNSHIP ORGANIZATION.

The idea has been suggested that the evils of township organizations in the city might be relieved by consolidating the three towns into one; but your committee think this would be "piling Pelion upon Ossa," for what could sixty thousand voters do at a mass meeting, either in electing suitable town officers or deciding by a *viva voce* vote the amount of revenue to be raised for the public uses of the town. Could not such meetings be controlled by a few hundreds of hired "roughs," who would be paid for their services out of taxes voted by themselves into the hands of their corrupt leaders, whom they would elect to office?

The power to increase the number of polling places in the township does not remove the difficulty, as it would be impossible in that case to get any fair expression as to the amount to be raised by taxation. A single moderator at each polling booth in a large city where every voter in the city has the right to vote at any polling place within it when consolidated into a single political township, could do but little, even if so disposed to prevent illegal voting. But when such moderator should be chosen by an organized band of "repeaters," as would be the case at many of the polling booths, there would be no protection whatever.

ADDITIONAL REASONS FOR CHANGES PROPOSED.

Having thus endeavored to comply with your instructions, your committee on taxation deem it proper to present a few additional reasons why some of the recommendations in their preliminary report should be carried out. The cost of the assessment and collection of city taxes for the year 1872 was

$89,416.99, not including office rent or any portion of the expenses of the law department. And it will be safe to estimate the expenses for 1873 at $100,000, with an annual increase for each succeeding year. All this would be saved to the taxpayers by adopting the plan suggested, of assessing all taxes upon the single valuation to be made by the proposed supervisor of revenue or county assessor.

There are of the city taxes since 1869, remaining unsettled, more than two and a half millions of dollars, of which at least two millions will never be collected; and that amount either has been taken, or must be extracted from the pockets of those who have already borne more than their full proportion of the public burdens.

The simplification of the assessments under the plan recommended, and the more equal distribution of the burdens imposed would, in the opinion of your committee, greatly reduce the number of tax contestants, and save to the city and county treasuries a very large majority of the revenues thus annually withheld and levied in succeeding years upon the property of the people who have already paid.

INDIRECT TAXATION NOT PRACTICABLE.

In the discussion which followed the report of September 26th, the plan for collecting all the taxes from the business of the county was urged as possessing many advantages over the one proposed by the committee. But, admitting that indirect taxation, if applied to the whole nation, might distribute itself with some approach to equity, still it would be difficult, if not impossible, to adjust such taxes so as not to impose an undue portion of the public burdens upon persons of limited means and restricted business. But were this system to be adopted by a single State, county, or city, a large portion of the whole tax levy would become a premium to merchants, manufacturers, jobbers, and traders of all classes who reside outside of the community in which the tax is collected, and to that extent would rest as a dead weight upon the taxed industries in their honorable race for supremacy. To cripple the business of any community, is at the same time to reduce the value of all fixed property within it, and to build up all values in rival communities not so oppressed. Your committee, however, think that exertion to cause every person, company, or corporation to pay taxes "in proportion to his, her, or its property" should not be abandoned or despaired of; but that constant, careful, and intelligent effort should be made to approach more nearly to this constitutional requirement.

RECOMMENDATIONS.

Your committee therefore recommend:

First—That steps be taken to secure the signatures of the required number of legal voters to a petition to the county Board, to submit to the voters of the county the question of the continuance of township organization; and

Second—That bills be prepared to be submitted to our next General Assembly, providing the necessary legislation to prevent any inconvenience which otherwise might result from the abolition of township organization, and to define the duties and term of office of the County Assessor in Cook county, in case the town system is discontinued, and for the repeal of "Bill Number 300."

It has already been shown how important it is to the complete execution of their plan that the proposed incorporation of our city under the general act be accomplished; but, as this matter is now receiving the earnest attention of the Citizens' Association, any further recommendation is unnecessary.

Respectfully submitted.

A. J. Galloway,
E. G. Mason,
Robert Law,
Committee on Taxation.

December 3, 1874.

www.ingramcontent.com/pod-product-compliance
Lightning Source LLC
LaVergne TN
LVHW020637110826
845149LV00004B/1255
9781418191016